...the love you for
you are. May you [...]
want in life. Be Happy!

Sharon Roth
Katherine Cooper
Valoy Maddock

Christ
and the
Inner
Life

Christ
and the
Inner
Life

Truman G. Madsen

Second Edition

BOOKCRAFT, INC.

Salt Lake City, Utah

Lithographed in the United States of America
PUBLISHERS PRESS
Salt Lake City, Utah

Contents

Preface   vii

The Preeminence of Christ   1
An Analysis of the Manliness
That Became Godliness

The Commanding Image of Christ   8
A Look at the Ways
We Look at Him

Christ and Prayer   15
Some Insights in
the Prayer of Enos

Twenty Questions   20
An Exercise of
Spiritual Introspection

Christ and Conquering Thoughts   34
Thoughts About Evil
and Evil Thoughts

Christ and the Sacrament   39
Reflections at the Garden Tomb
of The Resurrection

Ye Are My Witnesses   43
A Short Story
Based on 3 Nephi

Preface
to Second Edition

In the aftermath of a series of lectures a young lady with hurt eyes waited patiently. When most of the others were out of earshot, she said: "The one thing that makes sense to me in your lectures is that sin is death. I know something in me has died. How do I regain it?" I answered in only one word: "Christ." Her whisper was almost desperate, "But how?" Because I have heard that desperate whisper from many, and in my own heart, I understood.

Near the close of the book of Malachi the Jehovah of the Old Testament who was to become the Christ of the New promised, "Unto you that fear [reverence] my name, shall the Sun [Son] of Righteousness arise with healing in his wings; and ye shall go forth, and grow up as calves of the stall." (Malachi 4:2.) From his lips the promise came again at the end of his ministry among the receptive multitude in the Land Bountiful. (3 Nephi 25:2.) And again, at the beginning of the restoration of our day, this was one of the first about-to-be-fulfilled prophecies spoken from on high to a stripling boy-prophet. (Joseph Smith 2:36, 37.)

"With healing in his wings." The Hebrew root of *wings* is *kanaph*, which denotes extremity, or uttermost part; "healing," one might read it, "in his hands and feet." In another sense, by his own extremity — the most unfathomable time in a lonely place on the side of the Mount of Olives — Christ's healing and nourishing power were generated. It is, likewise, in our own extremity that we rediscover him.

But is Christ's way a way of sacrifice, self-denial and discipline? Or is it a way of adventure, fulfillment and joy? The answer to both of these questions is yes. Within each soul, as in his, it is both. The world is dying to righteousness and therefore to life. The Saints are dying to sin and therefore to death, "growing up as calves of the stall." One cannot experience the heights which Christ promises without knowing, by vicarious or actual experience, the depths. And repentance through Christ is complete when we would rather die (die physically) than sin (die spiritually).

In the conviction that we are, most of us, radically undernourished by his light and life and spirit, and that our need for that nourishment is continual and crucial, I have written these brief essays. Undergirding them all is the strongest assurance of my soul: Christ is indeed a matter of life and death.

TRUMAN G. MADSEN

MAY 1978

The Preeminence
of Christ

The convert who inspired this essay (originally pub-
lished in the Millennial Star) *is John Heidenreich, now*
deceased. Often he related how he and his wife sat, during
the period of their conversion, late into the night, saying
over and over again, "It is so awesome, so marvelous.
Christ is a personality." Here is an attempt to illustrate
this magnificent Mormon insight: that Christ is both the
revelation of God as He is and the revelation of man as he
may become.

"If I ever joined that Church [The Church of Jesus Christ
of Latter-day Saints] it would be for another reason: In their
midst Jesus Christ has a place of preeminence as in no other
Christian group."

So spoke a minister some years ago to other churchmen
who were discussing the "temporal achievements" of Mormonism. Today he is a Latter-day Saint.

What, I asked him recently, did he mean? He had been
for at least twenty-five years a careful student of the New
Testament, of theology and of history. He had voiced with
conviction the creedal statements that Jesus was "Very God,
God Incarnate." In prayer, in worship and service, all, he had
been convinced, "in His footsteps," he had not only been
captivated by the personality of the Master but had ex-

perienced, as he witnessed to his congregation, the Spirit of Him. Christ, he often said, was not just a theological concept, but a "daily walk, a fellowship, and a present help." What of this had he now abandoned, and what had he deepened? What, beyond it, had he discovered? What difference did it make?

As we quietly discussed things sacred, clarity of thought and purity of feeling seemed to combine. Though much, we both knew, failed to get into words, we came to "understand one another, and both [were] edified and rejoiced together." (D&C 50:22.)

This man had been pushed and pulled in the religious world between two competing conceptions. Neither had the full "ring of truth" to him, nor could he envision a combination or compromise of them. To take either of them seriously was, he felt, to dilute the events of Christ's life, particularly of Gethsemane and Golgotha, into mystery or meaninglessness.

At one extreme, Jesus Christ was viewed as substantially God the Father, the Triune God of Greek and Latin creeds. His earthly ministry involved all the contradictions of incarnation: the Immaterial became material, the Creator of man became a creature of man, the Non-spatial and Non-temporal became subject to space and time. Thus, though God and man would remain forever unlike, Divine Incarnation, by a miracle open only to the eye of faith, "reconciled" them. Today Christianity, either by its seven sacraments or by grace mediated through the biblical word, was supposed to achieve the end envisioned, salvation.

On this view Christ's "sufferings and death" were those of an Absolute Being. In spite of the paradoxical declaration (at the Council of Chalcedon) of *both* the Full Divinity and Full Humanity of Jesus, it was clear that ultimately the manhood of Jesus was only the clothing of his Godhood.

At the other extreme, Jesus was viewed as simply another man, unique in some matters of degree but certainly not in kind. He lived a remarkable, and at times inspiring, life. Like so many reformers of society, he estranged those he sought to aid; and he met death at the hands of the Roman authorities.

On this view Jesus' sufferings and death were tragic. The prayer of Gethsemane was simply an effort toward courage to face crucifixion. But events in the life of Jesus had little more significance than those in the life of Socrates. To talk of atonement, in legal, psychological, or spiritual terms, was to indulge in nonsense.

Unable, then, to deny that there was *something* divine about Christ, yet unable fully to believe that he came into the world either wholly God or wholly man, this man sought a more adequate answer.

The re-revealed insights of the restoration came to him, as to others, with a convincing power that was unspectacular but pervasive. He saw in these insights the drawing together of the truths of opposed conceptions, the overcoming of their errors, and a flood of light on the meaning of life, both of Christ's and of our own.

Jesus Christ was not God the Eternal Father. He was the preeminent *Son* of God. He was not "another man." He was the Firstborn in the spirit and the Only Begotten in the flesh. His past, which he had in common with God the Father, is the foundation of his role as Christ. To ignore or deny these insights would be to miss the power and promise of his mission.

Without detailing the vast effects of these promises, including the resurrection, let us focus on Gethsemane and view it through the manifestations of the Son of God in modern revelation.

Out of our own spiritual lack, our own darkness, there may be profound misgivings about the significance of Jesus' example and his relationship to us.

We may say, for example: "He was God from the beginning. He was not really akin to us." The truth is that he lived, as we lived, in the preexistent presence of the Father. He offered himself as the "Lamb slain from before the foundation of the world," and assisted in the organization of the earth. In these senses he was the greatest of all and was properly called God. But mortality was for him, as for us, a genuine second estate, a growth process, and in it

he received not of the fulness at first, but continued

from grace to grace until he received a fulness. (D&C
93:13.)

We say, "But surely he was not subject to the conditions
we face." The truth is that though by his divine inheritance he
had power over death, he was tempted in "all points" as we
are, yet without sin, suffering pains and afflictions and temptations of every kind. He did not "ascend up on high" until he
had

> descended below all things, . . . that he might be in
> all and through all things the light of truth. (D&C
> 88:6.)
>   Behold I am the light; I have set an example for
> you. (3 Nephi 18:16.)
>   . . . What manner of men ought ye to be? Verily I
> say unto you, even as I am. (3 Nephi 27:27.)

We say, "But because he did not violate the law of God as
we do, he does not know the burden of guilt and alienation."
The truth is that, because of his sensitive, uncompromising
submission to the Father's will, he was the only one of the
Father's family who did not transgress, who in no sense
deserved the throes of sin and the withdrawal of the Spirit.
Yet through his life, climaxed by those incomprehensible
hours in a garden beyond the brook Cedron, he suffered
"according to the flesh" (Alma 7:13) the pains and afflictions
of all forms of human evil-doing. He participated, voluntari-
ly, in the actual conditions that follow in the wake of de-
liberate transgression. He experienced the cumulative impact
of our vicious thoughts, motives, and acts.

We say, "But it was easier for him because of his divine
Sonship." The truth is that it was infinitely harder. He endured "even more than man can suffer except it be unto
death" (Mosiah 3:7), a suffering how exquisite and hard to
bear we know not, which caused him

> to tremble because of pain, and to bleed at every
> pore, and to suffer both body and spirit — and

would that I might not drink the bitter cup, and shrink —

Nevertheless, glory be to the Father, and I partook, and finished my preparations unto the children of men. (D&C 19:18,19.)

We say, "But he was never left unto himself, as we are." The truth is that few can comprehend his cry on the cross, "My God, my God, why hast thou forsaken me?" Who can fathom his reiterated statement in modern times,

[I have] trodden the the wine-press *alone*, even the wine-press of the fierceness of the wrath of Almighty God. (D&C 88:106. Italics added.)

We say, "But what he did twenty centuries ago cannot affect me now." The truth is that the Christ who *was* is the Christ who *is*. Out of his life came a full knowledge of righteousness and a full knowledge of the effects of sin. This means that no human encounter, no tragic loss, no spiritual failure is beyond the pale of his present knowledge and compassion, gained

according to the flesh — that he may know . . . how to succor his people according to their infirmities. (Alma 7:12.)

No act in all history has united intelligence, virtue and mercy in so complete an expression of love, a love which, even dimly glimpsed, will "draw all men unto him"; a love which underlies his present living roles as Mediator, Revelator, Savior, Redeemer, and Advocate with the Father.

We say, "But his glorious triumph has no bearing on my own." The truth is that, exalted now on high, Jesus Christ is he by whom "the life and the light, the Spirit and the power" are sent forth by the will of the Father. (D&C 50:27.) Through Jesus Christ, *we* may come unto the Father. The pattern ordained is a pattern which begins when the light of Christ is given to every man who enters the world. It leads, if it is honored, into the first principles and ordinances of the gospel. It includes sublime blessings — knowledge, glory and communion, love, joy and peace, blessings even of personal visitation — which transcend the highest aspirations of martyr or mystic and of enlightened souls in every age.

But beyond these we are promised,

> ... If you keep my commandments you shall receive of his fulness, and be glorified in me as I am in the Father; therefore, I say unto you, you shall receive grace for grace. (D&C 93:20.)

Moved, as few who have tasted of his Spirit and love fail to be, with "a broken heart and contrite spirit" we may walk the path whereby to become, as President David O. McKay repeatedly testified with Peter, "partakers of the divine nature." (2 Peter 1:4.) As Christ was begotten of God the Father both in spirit and in body, so by being begotten of Jesus Christ through his laws and ordinances we may be transformed into a like condition of complete fulfilment, sons of God in the fullest sense, *like him.*

> Wherefore, all things are theirs, whether life or death, or things present, or things to come, all are theirs and they are Christ's and Christ is God's.
> And they shall overcome all things. (D&C 76:59, 60.)

Whatever else the "preeminence of Jesus Christ" means (and it means much, much more), this is the heart of it. Today, in testimonies of living witnesses and the radiance of lives endowed with his power, in the spirit and operations of his priesthood, and in the covenants and ordinances of his holy temples, the drama enacted in the land of Palestine is conveyed to our souls. As his sufferings and death brought man nearer to God and to each other, so individually, as we seek to comprehend him, he brings us ever nearer the realization of our own spiritual destiny, that the light in us may grow "...brighter and brighter until the perfect day." (D&C 50:24.) No hour of life need be so despairing or so exalting as to blot out his voice:

> Listen to him who is [your] advocate with the Father, who is pleading your cause before him —
>
> Saying: Father, behold the sufferings and death of him who did no sin, in whom thou wast well pleased; behold the blood of thy Son which was shed, the blood of him whom thou gavest that thyself might be glorified.
>
> Wherefore, Father, spare these my brethren that believe on my name, that they may come unto me and have everlasting life. (D&C 45:3-5.)

The Commanding Image
of Christ

The fable which introduces this chapter was originally presented at a devotional assembly at BYU. The central point is that honest doubt about spiritual realities must be open, else it becomes blind dogmatism; or, in other words, that darkness can only be removed by light. The related theme: until our image of Christ is compelling, until we rid ourselves of the images in our heads which make him a colorless, weak and, as one said, "vanilla-flavored" dreamer, we will not respond to his will. Hence the title "The Commanding Image of Christ."

Aware of the contrast of light and darkness, I sat down one day and wrote a fable. Have a little fun with this, because all too soon I am going to be very serious. It is entitled "The Sunstriking Fox."

Once there was a young fox who lived on the dark side of the moon. He associated with the other young foxes and took for granted their outlook. They claimed to be influenced by a moonlike orb on the other side called the Sun. No one had devised a way of traveling there, but some testified of visionary glimpses. And all claimed to be subject to its warmth.

Eventually the fox went away to school. When he came back he was often seen talking to himself. That, on good authority, is normal for most foxes, in school or out. One of his friends followed him around until he knew what he was down to. The monologue went something like this:

"All this talk of sunshine is really moonshine. I am going on a sunstrike. I will dig a hole way down. Then I will say, 'I don't know.' If anyone tries to argue I will say, 'No young fox knows.' And if they push me I will say, 'No fox *can* know.' "

He had no more than finished his hole than his friend came up, or, rather, down.

"What do you mean," he began, "no fox can know about the sun?" He had to say it loudly three times, because when someone is that deep in a hole it is hard to hear.

"Just that," the fox replied. "Foxes are using the word 'Sun' and no one even knows what it means."

"Interesting," replied the friend. "But that means *you* don't know what the word means . . . "

"All right," said the fox. "What I am saying is that I don't think anyone, especially *young* foxes, can know about 'the Sun.' "

"I see," said the friend. "How do you know that no *young* fox knows?"

"They just don't," the fox replied. "They just think they know."

"A remarkable assertion," the friend replied. "To be sure of that, or even fairly sure, you must have looked up all the young foxes. That is quite a fox hunt."

"No," said the fox. "I haven't counted all the heads in that way. Let's just say *I* doubt that they know."

"That brings us to you," said the friend. "Which is where, I believe, you both started and ended on this subject. You say you don't know."

"That's right."

"What would have to happen in your life to enable you to know?"

"I am not sure. But something that I can really see and that others can too."

"Very good," said the friend. "The Sun's *rays* are, if not presently seeable, at least presently sensible. But let us pursue *your* test. Convince me of your doubts."

"That is tricky," replied the fox. "But in the case of my doubts there is evidence that even *you* can see. I *act* as though I don't know."

"But do you admit that people with belief in the Sun can support their beliefs by action?" asked the friend.

"No."

"It is curious, then, that you should expect me to take actions as evidence of your doubt. But if action is the test, I have noticed that you do not live down to your disbeliefs. Last week I saw you reading a book on the delights of sunbathing. And hidden in your hole is a sunlamp."

"Well," the fox said, feeling a little sheepish in his fox clothing, "at least I am not psychological. I am not guilty of *wanting* there to be a Sun."

"Granting that wishful belief does not make a thing true, neither does wishful disbelief make it false. Where are we then?"

"Yes, indeed," said the fox, "where are we?"

"We are to this point," suggested the friend. "You are required to admit, after all, that there *may* be a Sun. But by your own tests I would say that as long as you stay under-ground you are not likely to come up with much evidence on either side. You are the cause of your own eclipse.

"Anyway, for all your expressed doubts you haven't yet been around enough to know that young foxes don't know, therefore not enough to know that no fox knows."

Moral: There are no atheists in foxholes.[1] (Though some may claim to be.)

Now I want to talk seriously about the sun. Modern revelation tells us that Christ "is in the sun, and the light of the sun, and the power thereof by which it was made." (D&C 88:7.) I would remind you that your 20-20 eyes, of whatever color, are no good without light — *no good at all.*

There are three great statements that the Living Christ has made of and about himself in our generation. I would like

---

[1]Truman G. Madsen, *Fables on Foibles, For This Time of Your Life* (Amherst, Massachusetts: New England Youth Conference, The Church of Jesus Christ of Latter-day Saints, August, 1964), pp. 18-20.

to submit them to you with an example or two and then bear witness.

Christ's Intelligence

One is the staggering statement, "I am more intelligent than they all." (Abraham 3:19.) The late B. H. Roberts took that to mean that Jesus the Christ is more intelligent than all of us together — all of the inhabitants of the human family in this world and in all of the multiple worlds of which Christ was Creator.

Whether or not that be the correct reading, one thing is clear, that somehow — and it is the nature of that "somehow" on which I want to dwell — Christ came to a "fulness of the glory of the Father." (D&C 93:16.) The glory of God *is* light and truth, or in other words, intelligence. (D&C 93:36.)

But how? Are you aware that in one experience the Prophet had, the Master approached him and said, in substance, "Joseph, I want you to read this. Then I want to tell you why I wanted you to read it. It is something John wrote about me." What does it say? It says something which is blasphemy in relation to the creeds of Christendom. Therefore, so much the worse for the creeds. Its says, "He (Christ) received not of the fulness at the first." He became what he became — and it says it three times. But he was called *the Son* of God because he received not of the fulness at the first, but "continued from grace to grace until he received a fulness." (D&C 93:12, 13, 14.)

Now we leave that context and refer to another one, this one from the witness of a man who considered himself hopeless, a man who knew the *Angst* of life (the German word that means more than anxiety), a man who had said at one point that he yearned for his own extinction. He didn't just want to cease to suffer; he wanted to cease to be. But something happened to Alma. And talking about it later to one he loved, his son, and others, he said he knew that though Christ could have looked upon mankind with the aid of the Spirit to behold what we are suffering, that wasn't enough. He (Christ) forever left the realm of spectator and entered the realm of participant. And, says Alma, he suffered in the flesh pains and afflictions and temptations of every kind. (See Alma 7:11,

13.) And any theology which teaches that there were some thing he did *not* suffer is falsification of his life. He knew them all. Why? That he might succor, which is to say comfort and heal, this people. He knew the full nature of the human struggle.

At this point a very large issue weighs us down and distorts the commanding image of Christ that we would otherwise have. It is this: "Yes, he may have overcome the world and temptations, but he does not know the meaning of failure. He does not know what I know — which is alienation, anguish, and knowing that the light has been withdrawn and that I deserve to have it withdrawn. These he does not know because he lived a sinless life."

But in modern revelation he has answered that.

I would like to tell you of one of the settings of the answer. It was within four walls, ironically named Liberty Jail, where the Prophet Joseph Smith spend four months without liberty — one of the few times (if there were any) when he was in despair. Much has been said of his physical suffering. It was terrible. But it is nothing compared to what he suffered inwardly, in the consciousness that his people were being whipped, house-burned, raped, and driven mercilessly, and he could do nothing — not even write to deny the faith by saying, "Forget Mormonism and go back home and refuse the word."

He said at one point, "If I had not gotten into this work I would back out, but I cannot back out. I have no doubt of the truth."

That sure conviction cost him the helpless awareness of hundreds upon hundreds of Saints in misery.

He cried out, and you know the answer. I select only this much: "If thou art called to pass through tribulation, . . ." and there continues a series of "ifs." (D&C 122:5.)

I cannot help recalling that that is the way the adversary taunted the Master: "*If* thou be the Son of God. . . ." (Matthew 4:3. Italics added.)

All of these "if" clauses in the description of Section 122 were fulfilled in fact:

... If they tear thee from the society of thy father and mother and brethren and sisters; and if ... thine offspring, and thine elder son, although but six years of age, shall cling to thy garments, and shall say, My father, my father, why can't you stay with us? Oh, my father, what are the men going to do with you? and if then he shall be thrust from thee by the sword,

... know thou, my son, that all these things shall give thee experience, and shall be for thy good. (D&C 122:6, 7.)

Joseph might not have been able to believe such a statement from a distant observer, but then the Master said: "The Son of Man hath *descended below them all*." (D&C 122:8. Italics added.)

In Gethsemane he knelt and endured all the feelings that you have had or can have in the blighting experiences of this world, "that his bowels might be filled with compassion."

Christ's Power of Light

The second great statement of and about Christ is from modern revelation: "That which is of God is light; and he that receiveth light, and continueth in God, receiveth *more* light. (D&C 50:24. Italics added.)

More light! We have light that enables us to see objects here, but the light of Jesus Christ lights the *subject*. It illumines minds and spirits — yes, and bodies. Listen to his promise:

And if your eye be single to my glory, your *whole bodies* shall be filled with light, and there shall be no darkness in you; and that body which is filled with light comprehendeth all things. (D&C 88:67. Italics added. Compare D&C 84:33; Luke 11:34-36.)

Then elsewhere in the scriptures we find the third great statement by Christ.

Christ's Nature As Our Destiny

"The day shall come when you shall comprehend [it does

not just say apprehend] even God, being quickened in him and by him." (D&C 88:49.)

Men have stood at pulpits and elsewhere — great men — and have testified that their knees have never buckled, that as one said of another, "He had nothing to hide." We have had monumental men who did not need redemption as much as they needed power, and who never fell very far from the communing light of which I have spoken. I cannot bear that kind of testimony. But if there are some of you who have been tricked into the conviction that you have gone too far, that you have been weighed down with doubts on which you alone have a monopoly, that you have had the poison of sin which makes it impossible ever again to be what you could have been — then hear me.

I bear testimony that you cannot sink farther than the light and sweeping intelligence of Jesus Christ can reach. I bear testimony that as long as there is one spark of the will to repent and to reach, *he is there*. He did not just descend *to* your condition; he descended *below* it, "that he might be in all and through all things, the light of truth." (D&C 88:6.)

If only one person who reads this can feel what I feel of the Spirit of God as I bear witness to the truth, this book is worth the effort.

Christ and Prayer

We all have a crying need for intimacy in prayer – to be "on the level," to stop pretending. Such prayer is self-revealing. But it is also Spirit-giving. And "he that asketh in Spirit shall receive in Spirit" (D&C 46:28), the Spirit of Christ. We pray "in his name" as we pray through him, and with him.

Yearning Prayer

They say it in one way or another, those who really know about prayer: Only yearning prayer gets through.

But there are three kinds of yearning.

We yearn when we mean what we say. But is that enough when we are asking the impossible, or when what we are asking is, if we could only see, not for our good?

We yearn when we care terribly. But is that enough when what we care for, however desperately, is a fist-shaking fixation that presumes God visions less of what is needed than we?

We yearn, finally, when we do not only mean and care intensely, but when at the core we are as anxious to listen as to ask. We yearn when we will to abide counsels already given and to respond to him and his way *in* his way.

So long as we are set in our uninspired desires, not

moldable, we must break our hearts before we can pray from them. So need we wonder why the heavens are often like brass over our heads?

Humble prayer is the beginning of communion with the highest of personalities — God and his Son Jesus Christ — of higher ways of seeing and feeling, as it were, through their eyes.

Achieving this is a life-process, not a five-minute thing. But it is sometimes closer in youth than in maturity. Youth may keenly grasp the truth: that even at our best we are like the blind boy who walks with his friend. He does not believe, nor bluff, that he is self-sufficient. Instead, he responds to the slightest nudge. (If you would know the power of God, try, early in life, to become just this dependable in your dependence.)

As this happens, the whole being becomes the instrument that vibrates upwardly. No special words are needed, no forced tone of voice, and no dramatic play-acting.

Then we begin to recognize the "first answers" to our prayers — the answers that always come before the others.

What are these?

They are subtle flashes that register within. And they are real. They center "in your mind and in your heart" (D&C 8:2) and are, therefore, a perfect blend of thought and feeling. They come with a serene flow of power that is light and warmth and liquid surety. They whisper a "Yes," or a "No," a "Wait," or a "Be still," a "Trust," or an "Act well thy part."

This is what a modern young prophet calls "breaking the ice" and "obtaining the Holy Spirit" which cause "the bosom to burn." He says that much emptying ourselves of unworthiness and much filling ourselves with concentration precedes it. He says we should strive to stay on our knees until it happens.

And how do you know that this burning is of God? Maybe it is just hope, guess, or wish.

You know by the quiet verdict of your own inner being. (And you know just as well when you don't know.) You know because the haunting "I doubt" and the painful "I fear" are swallowed up in living light. You arise this time, after many darkened times, tinctured with gratitude. With the glow comes a lingering love, a knowledge that forges resolve to do what must now be done, and a faith for next time.

Thus yearning prayer becomes burning prayer — burning-with-the-Spirit prayer.

Happy is the youth who prays for, and then until, and finally with, this subtle flame. For "he that asketh in Spirit shall receive in Spirit." (D&C 46:28.)

Facets of Prayer

My point is simple. The "how" of prayer is both the hardest and the easiest thing in the world. Enos proves it.

My inspiration is simple: I know a lot of twentieth-century lads just like Enos.

One afternoon Enos went to hunt beasts in the forest. He was not long in the wilds before he forgot all about hunting. He forgot because he began remembering. " . . . The words which I had often heard my father speak concerning eternal life, and the joy of the saints, sunk deep into my heart. And my soul hungered." (Enos 1:3, 4.)

He went to his knees and began to cry unto God for relief from his backlog of evasion and cover-up.

How long did he pray? All the day long and on into the night. What could he possibly say in all that time? He tells us that his prayers were "many long strugglings," a searching and exposing of his own depths, a pouring out of his "whole soul."

The answers (and they came in what a present-day apostle calls "finished sentences") overwhelmed him. "Enos, thy sins are forgiven thee." (Verse 5.) He prayed on, and still on, for those he loved, for reassurance about the future. And when testimony came, here too he "knew that God could not lie; . . ." (verse 6), "wherefore [his] soul did rest" (verse 17).

And he returned home.

So what was unique about Enos's prayer?

The Hidden Self

It was a "wrestle which I had before God," a pouring of his real self into the cups of his words. But it was more than that. At one level we all indulge the daily cliches and more or less "mean" them, — "forgive us, help us to overcome our weaknesses." At a deeper level we voice actual present feelings, even when they are raw, ugly, miserable ones. "Father. I feel awful — I am racked with anxiety." But there is a deeper level, the inmost, which often defies words, even feeling-words. This level may be likened to what the scriptures call "groanings which cannot be uttered." Turned upward they became the most powerful prayer-thrust of all. There *is* a wordless center in us.[1]

Such, we may be sure, was the tone of Enos's prayer through those long hours. He learned that when we break the veil to our deepest self, we also penetrate the veil of heaven.

Faith in Christ

Some might say, "Well, maybe Enos just had more faith than the rest of us; most likely he was gifted that way — naturally religious."

Look more closely.

His words suggest that he was surprised to learn he had *any* faith. He knelt, mostly convinced of one thing: a weighty mountain of his own great need. That kind of mountain, incidentally, only faith can move. After many hours of pleading and receiving, he was in awe. "My guilt was swept away" (verse 6), he says. He did not doubt that it was gone. But marveling he cried out, "Lord, how is it done?" (Verse 7.)

Note the puzzling answer. "Because of thy faith in Christ, whom thou has never before heard nor seen." (verse 8.) It was true he had not seen Christ. But he had heard *of* him in the living words of his father.

But notice also that the instant he had a directing touch from the Lord, it brought a staggering inner influence. "My faith began to be unshaken in the Lord, . . ." (verse 11), he writes. Thus kneeling there, the mustard seed became a tree!

There is, in all of us, an eternity more of faith in God than we tap. Kneeling to reach for faith we may find we are reach-

---

[1]"We know not," says Paul, "what we should pray for as we ought; but the Spirit itself maketh intercession for us with groanings which cannot be uttered." (Romans 8:26) The Prophet Joseph changed "groanings" to "strivings." Thus we can through the Spirit pray wordlessly and soundlessly.

ing *with* it. That, Enos shows us, is another facet of real prayer.

Enos's response was total. He did not run away holding his ears. We have the hindsight (the record is clear) to know that Enos became a lifelong dynamo, that he was "wrought upon by the power of God" (verse 26) unto the end of his days and that he "rejoiced in it above that of the world" (verse 26).

That performance demonstrated the foresight of God. Surely the Lord knew the real Enos — that he had it in him to use divine power as the Lord himself would use it. That enabled the Lord to answer Enos without reserve. It must be a different problem for the Lord to answer cool, bargaining, curious, all-talk-and-no-listen prayers.

And isn't it true that, unlike Enos, we pray for God to change everything — except us?

We hear much today about an identity crisis — the ache that comes when one begins to ask in a lonely, anguished way, "Who am I? What do I really want?" A lot of fuzzy answers can be given. But what is needed is a change of question. If you are, as I happen to know, an embryonic Enos, then you can kneel in some forest or other and ask from the center of you, "Whose am I?" And I testify that when you expose your hidden self and latent faith and when you honor the quiet voice with total response, you will make a double discovery — yourself and God.

That is what prayer is all about.

Twenty Questions

"Reflect often upon thy past," is one of the profound counsels of patriarchs. The very remembering of spiritual things becomes, in a measure, a reliving of them, an antidote to dark days and self-doubts and a quiet form of worship. "Twenty Questions" was given at a summer school devotional at BYU. All will answer some of these queries with a "Yes." My hope was (and is) to evoke in the reader not just answers, but deeper and more personal questions like these about the influences of Christ in the life of the Church.

Some years ago on my return from the East, just after finishing my Ph.D., I had a phone call. A voice I hadn't heard before said, "Is your name Madsen?"

"Yes."

"You just finished your graduate work?"

"Yes."

"Was your field philosophy?"

"Yes."

"Philosophy and religion?"

"Yes."

"Are you still active in the Mormon Church?"

"Yes."

"How come?"

I played dumb, which isn't too hard for me sometimes, and said, "What do you mean, how come?"

"Well, anybody who has studied as you have — I don't see how you get these things together."

I said, "I'll be happy to talk to you about it." So he eventually invited me to dinner. It turned out — and I do not want to tell you too much about him because you might know him — that he was a fairly prominent young man who had graduated from a university which shall remain nameless, and that while at the university he had become seriously disturbed. He was now married, and, as we say, "married in the temple." He was curious still and wanted to know if there was a way of reconciling his former faith and his new discipline.

Well, it was an interesting evening, and it was not until we had spent nearly an hour merely sparring that I suggested we do something else. I said: "Look, I think we can get to the root of this if I ask you some questions and if you answer them with a simple yes or no. In advance, you should be aware that the questions are designed to see if you have really been subject to the dynamic currents of the Church. I think it will be easy for you to say yes or no. All right?"

"All right."

So began a series of questions, about twenty. He answered seventeen of them, "no," two of them, "maybe," and one of them, "yes."

Of But Not In

When we were through I said, "Well, now in all candor, if I had been on the witness stand and had been pledged to tell the truth, the whole truth, and nothing but the truth, and if those same questions had been put to me, I would have had to say yes to about eighteen of them. So the difference between you and me is not so much the various enterprises we have studied or sought to master in the world; the difference is that I have had some experiences that you haven't had. And that means that actually you are not about to leave the Church, as you say. You have never really been *in* it!"

Well, he resented that and told me that he had several standard quorum awards and other such "gold stars on his forehead" as evidences of being really *in*.

But I said, "No, the Church's flowing powers have not *really* been *in* you, whatever the geography of your Sunday afternoons."

Some Questions

I have made an outline list of those queries I put to him. I intend to ask them of you as perhaps a fruitful way of looking at yourselves.

Prayer

First about *prayer*, "Have you ever prayed and been lifted beyond yourself, both in the manner and in the content of your expression, so that it became more than a dialogue with yourself?"

He said no. He admitted that he had said prayers, though not recently; but so far as he could remember, he knew of no instance in which he was sure he was talking to anyone other than himself.

President Heber C. Kimball told his children that unless one feels before he finishes his prayer a certain wave of the Spirit of God, a certain burning in the center of the self, he can be fairly sure that his prayer is not heard under ordinary circumstances. If we apply that to our own prayers, I, for one, have to acknowledge a good deal of barrenness. But if any of your prayers are in that burning category, thank God and keep praying.

The Sacrament

About *the sacrament*. "Have you ever had the experience that Elder Melvin J. Ballard describes, 'feeling the wounds on your soul,' being soothed, being filled with the Spirit that warms, and thus being quickened in a hunger and a thirst to return to the sacrament table where you find healing? Has it been as if you were taking hold of a couple of electrodes and were subject to a current?"

He said, "No, I have always found sacrament meetings quite boring."

A Patriarchal Blessing

About a *patriarchal blessing.* "Have you ever had what President McKay would call the 'thin veil' experience? When a patriarch made promises to you, declaring your heritage and something of the promise of your destiny, was it as if you were surrounded by glorious, but somehow less tangible, persons?"

On that one he said, "Well, yes, I do acknowledge that I felt something; but I have since concluded that it was just my own wishful thinking."

The Scriptures

About *the scriptures.* "Have you had the 'before and after' experience of Joseph Smith, who speaks of reading the scriptures after receiving the gift of the Holy Ghost? He was astonished, looking back and comparing the experience with his previous readings:

> Our minds [his and Oliver Cowdery's] being now enlightened, we began to have the scriptures laid open to our understandings, and the true meaning and intention of their more mysterious passages revealed unto us in a manner which we never could attain to previously, nor ever before had thought of. (Joseph Smith 2:74.)

"Another way of saying it is: There are times when the scriptures can leap up off the page and bomb you, hit you between the eyes and, as it were, between the ribs such that you know these phrases were written under inspiration, and you see clearly how they apply to you."

It was Brother Marion G. Romney who told of reading with his son, in the upper and lower berths of a train on one occasion, taking turns — a verse at a time. After a while, he read a verse and his son was silent. He assumed his boy had gone to sleep. But a little later his son said, "Dad, do you ever cry when you read the Book of Mormon?" Brother Romney said, "Yes, son, there are times when the power and light of this book so permeate me that I find myself in tears." His son replied, "I guess that is what happened to me tonight."

Well, if we have been awakened in that way — he said he had not — then we are not one of those who have read the Book of Mormon up to the Isaiah passages and quit. I have sometimes wished that the book could be reordered, starting with Moroni, then Ether, and maybe Third Nephi, and then moving on. I am afraid that there are hundreds of thousands in the Church who have been hung up on the Isaiah passages and missed the treasures.

Ordination

About *ordination*. "Have you ever, in receiving the priesthood, or an office within it, or a calling to serve felt what President Stephen L Richards calls an 'essence of power,' or what Elder Orson F. Whitney calls 'liquid fire,' or what the Prophet himself spoke about as 'virtue' which somehow passed from the person into you?"

He said, simply, no.

An Instrument

"Have you ever been involved at the other end, *being the instrument* for setting apart or ordaining or baptizing or confirming? Moroni records the words of the Savior that, after calling upon God in mighty prayer, 'ye shall have power that to him upon whom ye shall lay your hands ye shall give the Holy Ghost.' (Moroni 2:2.) Have you ever had the experience of thus being a vehicle?"

"No, I have stood in a circle or two, but I would say it was a sort of mumbo-jumbo of remembered phrases."

Testimony

About *bearing testimony*. "Have you ever stood up, not simply to express gratitude, which we often do, and not simply to parrot the trilogy of phrases (about the reality of God, the sonship of Christ, the prophetic mantle among us) that we often use, but stood up because there was an almost compulsive lift to stand? Did you have the sensation of being, as it were, outside yourself, listening to yourself, when your words came with a transparent clarity, running ahead of your ordinary thinking; and you felt the core of your soul coming to the fore with a glow of unqualified conviction?"

He said, "No, I have occasionally 'borne my testimony' but I did not have one really. I was just using the words."

"What about," I asked him, "others who have spoken in your hearing? Has there never been a case in a classroom, or in a meeting, or in a conference, have there not even been instances when you have listened to the 'living oracles' at the head of the Church, when you were sure the person was speaking beyond his natural ability, when *the power of his testimony* seemed to cut through all the fog and go directly to you?"

"Beyond His Natural Ability"

I could have recalled the incident of President Heber J. Grant, who saw his brother enter the Salt Lake Tabernacle many years ago. His brother had been everywhere except in the Church, around the Horn, in mining camps, and oil fields. He had come to the point of suicide and then received, in ways I cannot detail, a strong feeling he should contact his brother, Heber. Well, he stumbled into the Tabernacle. President Grant did not know that he would be called on to speak, but he prayed that if he were he could say something to touch his brother. But he thought perhaps he had better check a reference or two. He pulled down his ready reference and began to look through it desperately. He wanted to speak beyond his own natural ability and so prayed.

Well, he was called on. He soon forgot that ready reference and simply bore his testimony to the power of Christ that led to the Restoration and that led the people of this Church across the plains. Specifically he bore witness to the prophetic glory of the Prophet Joseph Smith.

I have read that talk. There is nothing, as far as I can find, that is distinctive or unusual about it — it is on the surface a fairly ordinary collection of words. But when he finished and sat down, he heard George Q. Cannon quietly say, "Thank God for the power of that testimony." And President Grant bowed his head and wept.

Brother Cannon was asked to speak. He stood up and said, "There are times when the Lord Almighty inspires some speaker by the revelations of his Spirit, and he is so abundantly blessed by the inspiration of the living God that it is a mistake for anybody else to speak following him, and one of those occasions has been today, and I desire that this meeting be dismissed without further remarks." And so it was.

I will paraphrase somewhat the event of the next day when President Grant's brother came and said, "Heber, I heard you yesterday. Heber, *you* can't speak that well. You spoke beyond your natural ability." He used the exact phrase.

President Grant, who was pretty stark in his response, said, "Does the Lord have to get a club and knock you down? What does it mean when you know I can't speak that well when I talk about the Master and Joseph Smith?"

His brother said, "You win." He became an active Latter-day Saint and a powerful speaker in his own right. (Heber J. Grant, *Gospel Standards,* comp. G. Homer Durham [Salt Lake City: *The Improvement Era,* 1941], p. 369-370.)

That kind of experience, occasionally at least, should have happened to all of us. It had not to my friend or if it had, he had long since forgotten.

Spiritual Gifts

About *spiritual gifts.* The Prophet said, in effect, that no one has faith in Christ unless he has something along with it. "A man," he said, "who has none of the gifts has no faith; and he deceives himself, if he supposes he has." (Joseph Smith, *Teachings of the Prophet Joseph Smith,* comp. Joseph Fielding Smith [Salt Lake City: Deseret Book Co., 1938], p. 270; hereafter cited as *TPJS.*)

You can check the lists of spiritual gifts. There is one in Moroni 10, another in D&C section 46, and another in Paul's writings, 1 Corinthians 12. You can check, if you want more carefully to go through all the Doctrine and Covenants, and you will find about thirty different ways in which gifts are manifest.

"Have you ever had such a gift, especially in serving others? Have you ever sensed, say, the gift of discernment — the gift for the word of truth or knowledge — or the gift to teach it, or of wisdom or the gift to teach that?"

He said simply, "No, I do not believe in these mystical gifts."

Pure Intelligence

About the more specific issue, the Prophet's "flash of intelligence" phenomenon. "Have you ever received what the Prophet calls *'pure intelligence* flowing into you,' or a quickening in your soul that binds you to a truth or a person or a sacred place; a drawing power toward something or away from something that you cannot trace into your ordinary environment? Or have you ever just known by the spirit of prophecy that a certain thing was going to happen? I am not talking about wishes, guesses, hopes, hunches; I am talking about the phenomenon of *just knowing."*

Occasionally I have asked groups how many present have known at times, in *that* sense of knowing, that they were about to be called on to pray or to speak or to fill a particular office. All of these groups have ended up with two-thirds of the hands high, many others halfway up, not quite sure whether these "sudden strokes" came from a divine source or from somewhere else.

Again his answer was in the negative.

Music

About the voice of God in *music.* "Have you ever sung a hymn, or is there a single piece of music in this Church that speaks to your soul in the way the others do not — like for example, 'O My Father' with Crawford Gates's French horns and the Philadelphia Orchestra; or 'Come, Come Ye Saints' at its climax; or the Phelps 'Spirit of God' anthem?"

A girl was leading music in a sacrament meeting at BYU some time back. (Mormons cannot sing without a conductor; I have often marveled at that. Maybe it is symbolic of the fact that we believe the script, but there has to be a living person handling the script.) She was leading in a fairly perfunctory way the Eliza R. Snow hymn "O My Father." Then for the first time, I think she began to understand the words. This time they were given with power. As she led, she soon was not singing anymore and then was in tears. Somehow that was catching, it moved through the congregation. By the time they reached the last verse nobody was singing, or at least not with their voices!

Well, he said he had never had that experience. The words meant nothing to him.

Conscience

About the question of *conscience*. We do a lot to suppress and even distort our consciences. It is not uncommon in a standard course having to do with environment, whether it is psychology, sociology, or anthropology, to say that all you have when you talk about conscience is the residue of your early experience, some no-noes and yes-yeses. But conscience is not reliable, so goes the argument. Everybody has claimed the conscience for having done something that you would consider an atrocity, and then not having done other things that you would consider right, so it is very relative.

I am not sure of this; I tend to agree with the view of Parley P. Pratt — that is, if you will go far enough back in your memory (and this is difficult because you have closed it off), you will find that at age four or five your first approaches to temptation and sin were attended by a fantastic burning. "No," was the sensation, "no." And if you persisted that sensation became a fever. Then if you went ahead and did it, you felt an after-burning of guilt. Had you hearkened to that, according to Parley P. Pratt, and honored it, you would have increased in light to the present day. Instead, you have smothered it and written it off as just some sort of psychological illusion.

This is an intrinsic awareness — all of us have it. We are loathe to admit it to anyone, last of all to ourselves, but it is here, in the heart. And as the Prophet put it, it "gnaws at us," and it seems to be particularly unimpressed with any of the arguments that we can advance. It is as if it were deaf. We say, "I couldn't help it, it was bigger than both of us." "Everyone is doing it, nobody will find out." But conscience has wax in its ears; it does not respond.

Well, he told me that he thought "conscience" was a wholly ambiguous concept and that we would do well to eliminate it from our vocabulary.

The Temple

About the *temple* — he had been there. He was not too

impressed, or worse, he was impressed negatively. Someone had suggested to him in his earlier life that, in condemning "pagan ritual," Mormons were saying they did not believe in symbols. The person had also pointed out to him that what matters is conduct, not just sacramental acts. And so he was disturbed.

(We do a disservice to condemn ritual per se. There is nothing intrinsically evil about ceremony or ritual. It can be distorted. But so can everything else. It can become an end in itself, and we can and often do lose its power and its meaning, but neither of those are necessary.)

I asked him if he felt anything about the promise given at Kirtland referring to the House of God as "a place of holiness." I asked him if he was constrained to acknowledge as he entered the temple, regardless of the process within, that it was indeed "a house of glory, a house of order, a house of God." (D&C 88:119.) I asked him, in other words, if he had a feeling or *sense of the sacred*.

He said no, not at all, and he had no desire to return there.

I could have borne him the testimony of President McKay (but did not) to the effect that he was disappointed — the audience gasped when he said it, he, President David O. McKay was disappointed — when he first visited the temple. He gave us the reasons, and they are the ones that bother us: that it was over his head; that he did not distinguish the symbol from the thing symbolized; that he saw the human elements — people, different personalities — not all of them appealing to him; that he had very strange expectations, few of them fulfilled; and that he was not yet ripe in spiritual things. But I heard him say, at age eighty after having been in the house of the Lord every week for more than fifty years, that there were few, even temple workers, who comprehend the full meaning and power of the temple. I felt his witness to my core and decided I would reserve my misjudgments, keep quiet, and listen. I have learned — and absorbed — quite a good deal since.

Love

About *love*. How do you feel about this? Elder Matthew

Cowley said he had never lost a friend (he made up his mind in his youth that he wouldn't) over religion or politics. That is the Spirit of Christ. I think it is particularly needful in this Church at this time.

There is a spirit that can come to one who has tasted the flow of Christ's power that makes it impossible for a person to push you out of his reach. He may for the moment reject you, he may for years do so. But always you are there compassionate and concerned — unwilling, just because you disagree, to say, "I will never speak to you again," unwilling to breed distrust and suspicion, to nurture your own bad blood against him. If a person has not tasted that spirit, then by the Prophet's definition he has not yet begun to get close to Christ. For, said he, "The nearer we get to our Heavenly Father, the more we are disposed to look with compassion on perishing souls; we feel that we want to take them upon our shoulders, and cast their sins behind our backs." (*TPJS*, p. 241.) "Perishing" — that is a good word, it can mean a lot of things, any sense of perishing. When you find a spirit that wants to condemn, to attack, to pull down, you witness a spirit that is not of Christ. With love like his we are able to see others deeply, but seeing them, we are able to overlook the things that would otherwise antagonize us.

"I can't work with certain people," a man said once. He was being encouraged to do a task, a "dirty work" task, in his ward. "I can't work with these people, they're dumb, they're oafish, they're clumsy, they're not pleasant to work with."

And the person who had called him smiled and simply said, "Christ did."

The young man I was talking with found joy with only one or two of his Church associates.

3 Nephi 17

In summary, I asked him whether he responded with anything unusual in reading Third Nephi. That happens to be a transparent book for me. I have a friend who says that the most sacred chapter of the Bible is chapter seventeen of John. For me the most sacred chapter of the Book of Mormon is the same number, seventeen, in Third Nephi.

The Testimony of Jesus

I asked him if he had received *"the testimony of Jesus."* (See D&C 76:51-53.) I asked him if the most thrilling prospect of his life was not simply to imitate Jesus in behavior patterns, but *to become like him* in nature, in very attribute and appearance, and eventually, even through being begotten of him with all that means, *possessed of his power.*

He told me that he did not see the point of all this talk about Christ, and as a matter of fact, he doubted most of the theological utterances that Church members made about Him.

So much for the questions.

Living Water

I have not reflected my own grateful experiences in each of these dimensions. I have talked instead of past worthies. But I can bear you a testimony that these currents and many more are part of the flowing fountain of the Church. If we do not drink, if we die of thirst while only inches from the fountain, the fault comes down to us. For the free, full, flowing, living water is there.

"Come Ye to the Waters . . ."

Perhaps more often than any other, the question is repeated today, "Why aren't there as many spiritual outpourings today as there were in the first generation?" This is a very revealing question, because there *are.* But those who ask seem always to assume that their lack of experience applies to everyone.

It is like the person who comes in and says, "How do I know that I have a testimony?" In flippant moments I have occasionally replied, "If you have to ask *me*, you don't!" That is pretty harsh. But it is true.

The living water is with us. If anything, *more* is available today because of the varied and expanding opportunities of the Church. But it becomes actual only when the individual who seeks has a clear sense of the possibilities and is then willing to pay the price. I find any number of youths who are, as I was, very anxious to say what they would do *for* such blessings, but less anxious to say what they would do *with* them if they came. After a little introspection, we should not be surprised that the Lord is hesitant to entrust more to us than we can carry.

Several years ago I went to Jerusalem. A wall is still there, parts of it the same as anciently. East of the wall is a valley called the Valley of Cedron; there once was a brook that flowed down from it. East of that is a mount. It is called the Mount of Olives. And somewhere up on the side of that mountain — no one knows exactly where, though some profess to — there was a garden. Not the kind of garden you may have imagined, not a beautiful, flowered garden, but a garden of trees — olive trees. Into that grove, after he knew that he had to accept the will of the Father, and knowing what it meant, Jesus Christ took three of his disciples. And then he prayed alone.

The Power of Christ

I sat there and looked back at Jerusalem. You do not comprehend, I think, the fantastic power of the opposition of all kinds that he faced. You have been impressed in our generation with the war machines of the major nations. They are not comparable in any way, in lethal enmity, in ruthlessness, to what was beyond that wall. One walked into the clutches of Rome with the confidence you would have in the clutches of an octopus. Remember? Jesus did not answer all the objections of the learned, the canny, or the curious. In looking back and knowing what was ahead, he overcame them by his very life.

I say to you that when he said to the woman of Samaria and to others, "He that believeth on me, shall never thirst" (John 6:35); I say to you that when on the cross he looked down and back, under the searing sun, and said, "I thirst," he was reflecting both the promise and the need that all of us have. We, too, thirst until we ache. We, too, are living and dying on deserts. There is no alternative. Some of those deserts we are commanded to walk across without water just, I believe at times, to see what is in us. But when we struggle on, we find an oasis, and the living water, or what I have called the dynamic currents of the power of Christ. They flow into us.

A Testimony

I bear testimony that those currents are here. I bear testimony that the problem of reconciling this or that philosophy of religion with commitment is not as technical as we often make it. These problems are easily worked out when the mind is clear. The solution is simple: it is being alive, fully alive to the flow and power of the living Christ. When we are, everything is better; when we are not, everything seems dark.

May God help us to walk in the light; and, when we do not feel that we have it, to walk in the memory of it *with integrity*.

Christ and
Conquering Thoughts

---

*If there is a sense in which we are what we think, and
therefore inevitably the product of and accountable to our
thoughts, then we need the power of the Christ to make
such "weak things become strong unto us." The essay
below (originally printed in the* New England Advocate, *a missionary journal) is concerned with practical
ways of coping with unworthy thoughts.*

"My worst problem is that I have bad thoughts. What can
I do?"

Associated with the house of the Lord is the symbol of an
all-seeing eye.

It reminds us that Christ who lives is, as he told his young
Prophet, "a discerner of the thoughts and intents of the
heart" (D&C 33:1), and that as Paul says, "all things are naked
and open unto the eyes of him with whom we have to do."
(Hebrews 4:13.)

At first that is a frightening perception. We shrink from
it. We think about wanting "mountains to hide us." But when
we pursue it in depth, it is different.

Consider.

Are any of our conceivable evil thoughts beyond the
Lord? If so, would there be any sound foundation for trust in

him? How can a Christ who does not know or refuses to recognize our thoughts, one whose awareness is restricted to an utterly other realm of awareness, really help us now? This ethereal view of Christ (reinforced, I am afraid, by much traditional theology) also implies that venomous or unworthy thoughts could not be entertained by him during his mortal life, nor after.

But the power of his own voice in our era has brought that impotent idea to the ground. And thus given us power to rise above the ground.

He was "in all points tempted like as we are" (Paul), with "temptations of every kind" (Alma). How low then can we go in our thoughts? Not as low as he in the contemplation of evil. He was tempted through "the darkest abyss" and "descended below all things." Why? That he might be "in and through *all* things the light of truth." What? In and through *my* vagrant, aching, turbulent, unworthy thoughts? "Yes, my sons, yes." He has comprehended them all. His is the compassion of kinship. (D&C 88:6.)

A second flash.

An all-seeing personage sees all. That means that just seeing evil or contemplating it (however we may define evil) is not itself evil; that thoughts about evil are not necessarily evil thoughts. For Jesus Christ is now beholding the entire ugly spectrum of human experience. Is he therefore unholy? Was he in mortality? He is in a condition that enables him to "see through" all ideas, judgments and images to the truth.

Reread the oft-quoted passages about the thoughts. You will note that is not the occurrence of ideas in the head but their lodgment in the heart that degrades. "As [a man] thinketh *in his heart* so is he." (Proverbs 23:7. Italics added.) The issue is not so much what thoughts occur in our minds, but how we nurture them in our desires — what we aspire toward and recoil from. Some worthy men of God reached a point, so we are told, at which they could "only look upon sin with abhorrence." (Alma 13:12.) It was lusting (more than thinking) that the Master defined as committing adultery "already in the heart." He did not say lusting was identical with the act.

He *did* say that it was the beginning of it. "Suffer none of these things to enter *into your heart.*" (3 Nephi 12:29. Italics added.)

The heart, as the scriptures have it, is the combustion chamber of both the exalted and the degenerate drives in man's inner life, whether wrathful, envious, covetous, or erotic. Our minds may be bright and lucid in building idyllic palaces or contemplate, as the Prophet says, the darkest abyss. Our hearts settle the question as to whether something is good or bad. Therefore "blessed are the pure in mind" actually means "blessed are the pure in *heart.*"

It follows that what we call temptation really occurs in the life of the heart. If so, then so also must its overcoming. I submit that this is where we need Christ most and also where we admit him least. We think it sacrilege that he should somehow *leave* his throne and enter with us into the quagmire. Afterward we struggle to overcome it by not thinking about it. Thus we are driven in the wrong direction. We look down in shame instead of up in faith, while thought becomes intent, intent becomes obsession, and obsession carried out brings ashen despair.

What, then, is the way out?

Here are some standard and sometimes useful answers.

"Concentrate on work." Yes, but what do we do when feeling-drenched thoughts return? "Think of the consequences." Excellent, but when the pressure is really on, and we are blind to them, what then?" "Think of your mother, your honor, and the Golden Rule." Fine, but these often elude us. "Quote scripture," that helps sometimes. "Sing hymns to chase darkness." Good.

But what is ultimately needed, I witness, is something as dramatic (yes, and even traumatic) as the drama of life itself, an antidote as powerful as the poison. "He that *trembleth* under my power shall be made strong." (D&C 52:17. Italics added.)

Here, where it matters most because it is sacred and intimate, I can only be suggestive. But anyone who is buffeted will know what is involved. Who hath ears to hear will hear.

The atonement of Jesus Christ has unfathomed intellectual aspects. And it is astonishing how much time we spend (I do not say waste) struggling to get it through our heads, to understand it. But a beginning of real understanding is to stand under it, to permit his power to reach *beyond* our depths so that Christ's life can grasp, shake, and transform our own. *That* is the point at which we are living or dying.

So suppose a diabolical picture comes to mind, a thought of which we are ashamed (or is it the *feeling* we have toward the thought that makes us ashamed?). The force of it may blot out all that we ordinarily see and feel. Spiritual sensitivities are the first to go. We isolate this fraction of consciousness (I've got to have this out!), build up syrupy anticipation, convince ourselves that this is what we really want, and become numb to all else. Thus, it is fitting to speak of blind rage, blind greed, blind passion. In his *Screwtape Letters* C. S. Lewis has the devil say to a henchman, "It is funny how mortals always picture us as putting things into their minds; in reality our best work is done by keeping things out." We have forgotten that we would "always remember *him*" (which is more than remembering his teachings).

In such a moment of distress how can you pull him into your consciousness so that strength replaces weakness? I designate two ways from the prophets.

1. Picture Christ and remember how you are bound to him. In the crisis for example, when your temples thunder, imagine what you are tempted to do as if it were a large sledge hammer. See! See if you can stand at the cross and by this act or indulgence swing that hammer on the nail. That will break your compulsive pattern and restore enough to your consciousness to enable you to cry out and *mean*, "No!"

2. The other picture is positive. It is the more calm but daily vision to overarch all else.

It is the vision of the real-in-prospect.

Take, for example, carnal thoughts, the bubbling erotica which imbue our environment and, mysteriously, the subconscious. Ask yourself what you *really* want. But as you ask, invite and invoke your spirit, the deepest and best in you, and the Master's Spirit. Search with him for the vision of love and marriage that can claim your whole being, to include, but not end with, the chemistry of the flesh.

Such a vision will bring into focus a queen or king, an anticipation of the real thing. You will be inspired by your righteous thirst for such kinships and excitements. You will envision love that glorifies a pathway through the temple of God, and finally the culmination in which there is whiteness and joy.

Thus you take raw subliminal impulses that corrode. You sublimate (literally make sublime) them into conscious, desirable pictures. You light corroding fire with redeeming fire. And Christ who is the exemplar of all forms of godly love becomes the revelator both of your own possibilities in the world of affection and of the pathway that will make them actual.

Without such a vision the heart is sort of a mixer of cheap poisons for our veins. But with it life takes on a deep-breathing color of godliness. But isn't it sinful or at least impractical to have such visionary fantasies? Listen to Orson Pratt: "There is no danger of loving too much, but only of loving too little." Lurid, lustful desires are a form of the "too little." But the effulgent dream of godly love is "at the foundation of everything worthy to be called happiness."

You doubt? You fear to open up your own caldron to the Christ?

Then go on pretending, if you must, that there is a way to hide. But hear in the distance what, if you will, you can feel in the marrow of your bones. It is a contemporary voice the Lord expressed in the Doctrine and Covenants (6:36): "Look unto me *in every thought;* doubt not, fear not."

Christile and
the Sacrament

These reflections on the sacrament were presented to a Holy Land tour group as we visited in early morning the "Garden of Olives" (Gethsemane) and later held a special sacrament meeting at the "Garden Tomb" outside the ancient wall of Jerusalem and near the alleged place of crucifixion.

Perhaps the reason we have been given two set prayers for the sacred sacrament ordinance is that it is of paramount importance in this instance that we comprehend clearly what we are doing, what we are asking, and what we are promised in fulfillment of the conditions.

These prayers have been memorized by most of us. They are written in our heads and can be written in our souls as we hunger for the sacrament with the same constancy that fills our lungs with air.

The testimony of Melvin J. Ballard, a man I never knew personally, was, "I am a witness that there is a Spirit that attends the sacrament that warms the soul from head to foot. You feel the wounds of your soul being lifted." I testify to this reality also.

This ordinance — an ordinance that somehow connects with all other ordinances — is a way the Lord has given us of opening the portals of heaven. I know he honors it, just as he honors baptism or the laying on of hands. I know that when he spoke to one of the most righteous multitudes who have ever listened to his voice in this world (the Nephites), he taught them that through this pattern they could have direct communion with him.

The prayer petitions that we may "always remember *him*" (more than remembering his commandments). Sermons often suggest that we should think more consciously about him. That, I am sure, is true. But in a relationship of love, the beloved may not be every minute present in consciousness, but is in the hidden levels of awareness. Anything we do in a day has glory and meaning because under and over it all is our pull toward the beloved. Husbands and wives know. That is why Jacob could work seven years happily knowing that he would be given Rachel. That's why Nephi had the assurance of Christ, even while facing marauders and oceans and wilderness.

So we are always to remember him in our deepest motivations, in the core of our spirits. We are alive to his love in the deepmost part of us.

> And if ye do always remember me ye shall have my
> Spirit to be with you. (3 Nephi 18:11.)

He asks of us in the first prayer (the blessing of the bread) that we be *willing* to take upon us his name and that we be *willing* to keep his commandments. Maybe I am straining at the word. But that is a little different than saying, "We are now perfectly *able* to accept you and live as you would have us." We are *willing* after we have come to him and, as Paul says, "examined ourselves" stripped of all the facades. We have acknowledged our need. From the Old Testament prophets he required the offering of animal sacrifices. To us he has said, "I require only [and it is a real only] the offering of a broken heart and a contrite spirit." (D&C 97:8; 20:37.)

Any honest man who contemplates himself in the Lord's mirror is contrite; and submissive; and grateful to acknowledge, heart melted, that such spiritual blessings as he has are not all *earned* (except by this honest attitude of penitence), but have been given as a gift.

In the first prayer Christ asks us to remember *his body.* The great insight given through the modern prophets is that Jesus the Christ was indeed the revelation of God the Father. To know him as he is, a glorified personage, is to know the *exact* nature of the Eternal Father. That nature is officially denied by Christendom. Moreover, the Jesus Christ of the creeds (often pushed out of reach by doctrinal distortion) is shrouded in mystery by the notion that his physical presence is contained universally in the wafer and wine. No. We are to remember his body, and his body is glorified in space and time. More, it is the exact image of our own destiny if we will but glimpse it. Thus, the understanding of his glorification is the anticipation of our own. These emblems do not take his substance into them. The truth is unspeakably more. Because of these emblems and our inner attitude, his Spirit is *poured into us,* preparing us for his actual personal presence and the brightness of his glory. The human self is transformed; transubstantiation is, as it were, in *us.*

In the second prayer (the blessing of the water) we remember *his blood.* Why? Why blood? Is that not melodramatic? No. He is reminding us of more than blood from his side when someone threw or thrust a sword into him. More than the blood from the wounds in his hands and feet. He is reminding us of the blood that came from every pore of his body in those hours of the atonement, which to me are more inspiring than those on the cross. He is touching us with the power of recognition: that the blood he shed makes it possible for him to sanctify *our* blood. As modern revelation says, making us "clean from the blood of this generation." (D&C 88:138.) Clean means more than exonerated from the shedding of blood by men who have killed the prophets and the faithful. It means clean — sanctified — in our own bloodstream through his power. "The blood which was shed." Why? For himself? No. He would not have had to suffer thus for his own salvation. He could have received the presence of God the Father without it — note the wording, " . . . the blood of thy Son which was shed *for them.*" In an agony of compassion of which our worst pains are but a small taste, he bled for us.

> And he said unto them: He that eateth this bread eateth of my body to his soul; and he that drinketh of this wine drinketh of my blood to his soul; and his soul shall never hunger nor thirst, but shall be filled. (3 Nephi 20:8.)

It is thus that we are removed from the recognition of what he did to the reception of what he *now does* for us.

Ye Are
My Witnesses

Though fiction, this story is based on the narratives in Third Nephi. (It was printed first in the New England Advocate.*) It springs out of a concern that has haunted me ever since I began to understand the New Testament. What would Christ say, what would he do, what more of himself would he unfold if he were surrounded by persons whose love for him was as intense as the hate of those who crucified him? The Nephite multitude provided such a setting.*

Timothy, his ankles bound with leather, was a crumpled figure against the gray and merciless wall. Here, on the outskirts of the city, the fury of the mob was increasing. They were stripping him now, denying even the protection of cloth between him and the small stones they were throwing. Their pellets had been shrewdly chosen — sharp, cutting, intended by their size and speed first to torment, then to gash and bruise, and finally to kill. They wanted him to die; but he must die slowly, wincing and writhing. He would suffer until a rock to the temple or just above the eyes crushed his last breath.

Down the narrow roadway, behind a sagging wall of an abandoned house, Nephi, brother of Timothy, was watching.

His own life in jeopardy, he had followed the conspirators here, burning with indignation that they were violating the public pact of the Chief Judge: Stoning required the full review and sanction of the Zarahemla Governor. Yet here, now, were judges goading the mob to violence.

For thirty years, ever since the commission of their aging parent, Nephi and Timothy had labored in the cities of the land Bountiful, teaching and witnessing of the coming Messiah, repeating the prophetic saying of their forefathers. And in thirty years the hostility, even of some who first befriended them, had turned into murderous intent. Now, in a well-planned scuffle near Nephi's home, they had singled out Timothy for torture.

Nephi was watching, but then he could not watch. The ghastly spectacle of their leering faces, the off-blows of the rocks, the swollen face of his brother, the crescendo of their curses staggered him. In waves the terrible sense of his own utter helplessness went over him. He was unbelieving as he hid his face in his hands. Was it happening? Could it happen? Was he really here? And where was God?

For an instant there was a lull. Were they satisfied and would they leave Timothy wounded but alive? No. It was over. He knew from the sound of the mob. They were receding now, scattering to their preappointed places to establish their alibis. They would abandon the body for others to discover. The word would travel fast to the Governor, but not fast enough to bring any justice.

Sickened and reeling Nephi waited, waited for the silence that meant the street and his brother were abandoned. How long it took he couldn't tell. Time was strangely elusive. But with only the sound of his dust-muffled sandals on the roadway, and his uneven breath, he came to the limp figure. For a moment he felt revulsion and horror at the heap of stones stained with blood. He could only look by sheer will at Timothy's body, cold in death. Then, his eyes closed, and he sank to his knees and moved in a spontaneous gesture of his soul.

"Timothy," he murmured, placing his hands on his

head. "Timothy, in the name of Christ return to life. By his authority I command you to rise."

At the sound of his own voice his faith seemed to spring up anew. He sat back in a penetrating gaze. There was no motion. But he watched and waited with full expectation. Then it began. There was a stir in Timothy's lips, a flutter in his eye. He groaned and moved slightly. It seemed forever before his eyes opened and he looked up but without sight. "Timothy!" Nephi said, again the sound of a miracle in his voice. At last Timothy not only looked but saw. "Nephi!" he said.

Two years had passed since then. Reports of this miracle and of other manifestations of divine intervention were circulated throughout the land Bountiful. But they brought no one to faith. They were viewed by the lawyers and the learned and the luxurious as a legend to trick others into this delusion about Christ. "Obviously," they said, "Timothy had never died."

Like an evil wind, a secret political combination gained power. The Governor was stabbed in his chamber, several worthy judges were poisoned, and the civil government was in ruins. In every city the halls and courts of law were abandoned. The only order in the land grew out of families grouped for their own protection, many of them desperately afraid there would be bloodshed even among themselves. And the only unity was found among those who had made a secret pact in a Cain-like conspiracy to be "united in hatred" against those who continued to talk of the traditions of the fathers about a Messiah and the so-called "signs" of his coming.

To Nephi and his brethren this meant that there was little safety and less hope.

They were marked men. They could not so much as teach their children of the prophets without risk that one day, in a school or dooryard, someone would set off explosions of violence. Travel, for any purpose, was an open invitation to marauders who preyed upon the caravans and on each other. The house and family of any man who expressed belief in the prophets, especially Samuel, was threatened with fire or ransacking or something worse.

And as for the conduct of the people. A sodden, sensual syrup had filled them. Their learning was cunning, not wisdom, and that cunning insulated them from anything sacred. They were motivated by position, power, and riches. Few, terribly few, cared for honor. Rape was as common as drunkenness; and murder, as common as both.

Traveling in various disguises, meeting in caves and sometimes underground, Nephi and Timothy and a few others continued to testify. The baptism of repentance (which, in secret, they still read about in the accounts of "The Waters of Mormon") was given to those who were touched by the great power which attended their prophets' words. Sometimes when Nephi spoke there was such a demonstration of the Spirit of God in his testimony that none could disbelieve. Yet belief was followed, too often, not by love and prayer but by bitter anger. And even some who listened fell into the patterns of those who didn't, saying of the prophets:

"Some things they may have guessed right among so many."

"But it is not reasonable that such a being as Christ shall come."

"If so, why will he not be born in this land instead of the land abroad?"

"This is a deception of the fathers to keep us in ignorance to believe some great and marvelous thing."

"They want us to be slaves to their words."

"They want to possess our lives."

"They hide in ignorance, for there is no way that our own eyes can see that what they say is true."

Then came disasters.

One evening, as Nephi rose from a table and was turning around, the floor suddenly became a dizzying, rippling monster. There was nowhere to go, nothing to do. In a matter of seconds the children were nauseated and panicked. Convulsion after convulsion, each one worse than the last, tore away at every desire for relief. The family groaned as they crouched in doorways. Thunder and lightning, such as they had never seen, seemed to have entered the very earth, intent on destroying it and all life with it.

It was an ordeal such as even Nephi had not really foreseen. He had tried to picture how Jesus might be put death, to understand what the prophets meant when they spoke of Christ's suffering and death being signalized by tremors in the earth and leading to the exclamation, "The God of nature suffers." But this! Three hours for destruction to reign! And then darkness, thick suffocating darkness.

Nephi was soon to receive word that Gilgal and Jacob, large and notable cities, were utterly buried; that Onihah and Mocum had been swept into the tidal swirl of the sea; that fire and crags and gaping fissures had wiped out the people of Gad and Josh and Kishkumen.

In all, sixteen cities were either destroyed or gutted!

But while others mourned in abject misery, Nephi knelt with his loved ones and gave thanks, again and again, that his family had been spared! And his house! And the temple!

Around that temple in the land Bountiful the fugitive survivors gathered, to count the cost and recount the holocaust, gathered in response to Nephi's request to all the faithful.

And there, while they marveled, twenty-five hundred of them heard a voice from the heavens.

What had they expected? Nephi wondered as he listened. They had known the shock-power of earthquake; every one of them had been buffeted by the turbulent forces from without. Now they were to experience the far more moving power within which was neither loud, brash, nor dinning in their ears.

Instead, it was as if the earthquake and the fire and the lightning and the sea were pulled together into a liquid burning and then released into the marrow of their bones. It pierced their souls. To the depths of their aloneness and anxiety and estrangement and even despair it penetrated. And their hearts were on fire!

That was the beginning of a day that transcended Nephi's most inspired anticipations.

For as the voice spoke the third time, it was understood.

"Behold, my Beloved Son, in whom I am well pleased, in whom I have glorified my name — hear ye him."

The Christ descended before them and the multitude fell to their knees. He bade them arise and come forth. And they touched him. Then the Lord spoke to Nephi, calling him by name, and singled out eleven others who were to receive his ministry.

Through that entire day Nephi listened enraptured while Christ ministered with overwhelming power, and counseled and ordained, and expounded with a visionary sweep of all time at his command, and reviewed the prophets with breathtaking light and healed the sick one by one, and blessed their children, and then prayed with the entire multitude in a way that filled their souls with inconceivable joy.

Then as the multitude wearied, he promised to return to them on the following day and withdrew.

By morning the multitude had swelled. All night the report had been carried throughout the land. And many, even of the halt and injured, found ways to gather to the spot where Jesus had been seen and heard.

As Nephi stood in the early dawn and looked out over the multitude it was a strange, but welcome, sight. He saw persons almost faint from the effort to cross the rude bridges over swollen rivers and athwart awesome cracks in the earth; aged men and infirm women, strong and eager youths, mothers with child. He saw makeshift garments, shoes that did not match and some with no shoes at all. There were many small children, some, no doubt because parents were anxious to bring them, others because the memory of the earthquake made them cling to their families.

Nephi recognized the faces of many who had risked their lives to be baptized unto repentance, some he had not been able to visit for years. It was a reunion that melted his heart.

Nephi gathered the Twelve near the temple and instructed them to divide the expanding multitude into twelve groups. Each disciple was assigned a group to teach, reliving the experiences of the day before.

In his own teaching Nephi felt spiritual exhilaration. It was so real that it seemed unreal: That he should be here recounting to his brethren what it meant to him to kneel at the Master's feet and to recognize the prints of the nails in his feet! What it meant to embrace the Redeemer after he had opened his robe and led Nephi's right hand to the wound in his side. As Nephi spoke of his vivid remembrance of the teachings of the Master, there rolled through his soul the phrase of Alma, "O, then, is this not real? Yea, because it is light." All the heaviness of the past, the years of anguish were instruments of the light, a light that seemed now to defy gravity as well as disperse darkness. And the response of the multitude was almost smothering — no shouts of derision, no anger, no stones. There was faith here. And hunger for the things of God.

After the formal counsel, the Twelve went to the water's edge, and the multitude followed. Nephi fulfilled the Master's charge that they kneel in mighty prayer and seek the Holy Ghost. Then he took his brethren one by one, baptized them, and came forth out of the water.

As they emerged from the water the Spirit of God flowed down upon them. The multitude watched (did they all see it?) while an actual conduit of light and fire descended. It became, as it were, high noon at mid-morning. The moist air appeared as bright fire, and the quiet clouds and silent trees seemed a sacred sanctuary. And while they stood thus filled with the eternal burnings of high heaven, Jesus stood in the midst of them.

He commanded the disciples and the multitudes to kneel down again.

And then it happened.

They had been praying, only minutes before, to the Father in the name of Christ. But now Nephi and his brethren, lifted and lured by the divine fire, found themselves praying directly to the Lord Jesus Christ. "My Lord, my God," Nephi said in a barely audible voice. Gratitude and confidence and intimate rejoicing poured out of him.

In this act Nephi felt sure release. He had known the Spirit at times in his ministry, but not as he knew it now. In touch with the present personage of Christ, Nephi felt like his spirit enveloped his body, open to a flame that was both his

own and yet not his own. There was no labor to think of
words, no striving for their expression. Desire sprang up in
him from below all the surfaces of his nature. And he knew as
he prayed that he prayed according to the will of the Father.

He could not take his eyes from the radiant Christ who
seemed to stand between heaven and earth. Yes. Nephi knew
him. His superlative manliness and matchless tenderness
were beautiful, overwhelming. His height and nobility and
serenity and aura combined in his movements to make them
sublime. Nephi felt he was remembering what he had, in
some primeval awareness, known, as if his eyes were ap-
prehending now what his spirit had always intuited.

In a moment the Savior locked him in his gaze. And
Nephi sensed, felt, knew that he was being seen as he was,
that the pulsings and aches of his center self were clear to him.
Jesus was not looking at him but into his soul. Faith rekindled
in Nephi with the longing for complete worthiness in Christ's
presence.

As if by preappointment Jesus took a few steps from
Nephi and the kneeling disciples. Then he himself bowed to
the earth. With face upturned so that Nephi could see his
profile, he said:

"Father, I thank thee that thou hast given the Holy Ghost
unto these whom I have chosen; and it is because of their
belief in me that I have chosen them out of the world.

"Father, I pray thee that thou wilt give the Holy Ghost
unto all them that shall believe in their words.

"Father, thou hast given them the Holy Ghost because
they believe in me; and thou seest that they believe in me
because thou hearest them, and they pray unto me; and they
pray unto me because I am with them."

Witnessing these words from the lips of the Savior,
Nephi felt new flashes of intelligence in the prophetic writings that had become part of him. He could see now what he
had not fully seen before, the glorious answer to those who
said that the life and sufferings of Christ made no sense at all.

For here before him knelt the Son of God, the eminent
Son of all sons. One could read his life in his countenance.
Had he not lived through the frail hours of infancy? Had he

not known the fiery darts of mortal temptation? Had he escaped any of the struggle with the blood of the family of man, the blood which, without divine power, blasts man's dignity and turns evil into worse evil? None. And he had overmastered all! The glory of godliness now was his in magnificent justice. All of Nephi's strivings for worth were engulfed in this sacred moment.

Jesus arose and returned to his Twelve. In unison they continued to pray with steadfast assurance.

Then, as Jesus looked upon them, he smiled. And such a smile! As Nephi studied the lines and sweeping comprehension of that smile, he saw a transfiguring light. The Savior's face, his robes, his whole person seemed to become near-transparent, as if a coursing power of illumination had burst into brilliant flame. Through and through, his robe was white, his hair was white, not a blanched shade, but a living, fulsome, vivid white. And it was as if the place where he stood had been put at the center of a prism.

Wondering if others likewise beheld, Nephi turned to Timothy. And beheld that his brother and the disciples, all of them, were likewise aglow! They were transformed! In an instant Nephi knew that he too was full of this light, and that he shone above all brightness.

Thus enveloped, Nephi felt cleansed. A molten purging power along his veins and arteries seemed to heal him of the residues of his past and its poisons. He could taste the rapture of being clean. Purity was not numbness, he thought in a flash, but the ringing and singing of every fiber of his flesh. He almost choked in conscious aliveness.

Resolute, the Savior said to his disciples, "Pray on!" But Nephi only wondered how any of them could wish to cease.

Jesus went again a little way away and knelt.

"Father, I thank thee that thou hast purified those whom I have chosen, because of their faith, and I pray for them, and also for them who shall believe on their words, that they may be purified in me, through faith on their words, even as they are purified in me."

Then the Redeemer said:

"Father, I pray not for the world, but for those whom

thou hast given me out of the world, because of their faith,
that they may be purified in me, that I may be in them as
thou, Father, art in me, that we may be one, that I may be
glorified in them."

Again the Savior returned to his chosen ones and smiled
upon them. Then he returned to his kneeling place. "Father,"
he said. And then came words no human tongue could utter.

The language of Jesus soared beyond any Nephi had ever
heard in mortal life. Was it an unknown, a foreign tongue?
No, because he understood it at the core of his being. Yet he
did not know the words. He listened and it was as if the
expressions of the Master swallowed up distance and separa-
tion. Word, thought, and feeling were all one. A comprehen-
sive vision emerged through the tatters of the clumsy words
Nephi had learned to know and use. Such an outpouring,
such perfect grasp! It was the language of the Divine! From
the moment of its utterance, Nephi felt he had been ushered
into the presence of the Eternal Father.

Hearing and seeing in this way Nephi was pulled to the
inner love of Christ in what was, at the time, a flood of self-
awareness. He grasped (had he ever before?) the perfect bond
between the Father and the Son and the sons of men. Layers
of obscuring doubt and confusion were lifted away. It was
more than experiencing the Holy Ghost, more even than the
joy of its sanctifying power.

In the depths of him he was seeing a visual prophecy. For
in the prayer of the Christ he saw the visage, the visible
image, of Christ's eternal nature. He could visualize, picture
the personage of the Eternal Father. And in that comprehension he received the sealing testimony, the indelible promise
of his own glorification.

That was what Christ meant — "that they may be one in
me as thou, Father, art in me." He beheld it! The precious
promised transmission of the divine nature, from the Father
to the Son to the sons, by the lawful miracle of light upon
light.

He saw. And felt.

Then Jesus arose. This time as he approached the Twelve
there was an air of release in his step as if he, too, had been

measured and fulfilled, as if some long-waiting chord in him had found attunement. Nephi, studying the Savior's face, saw again, attended by transcending whiteness, the same expression of compassion as on the evening before when having healed so many children he had said, "Behold, your little ones." One of them was Nephi's. Named after Grandfather Alma, he was small for his four years. His left leg had been withered from birth. Many times the family fasted and prayed that Nephi might heal him. But though he had often blessed others, these efforts for little Alma were vain. The boy had never learned to walk even with a crutch. At his instant recovery under Jesus' hands, he and his sisters had danced a circle of joy, hugging and tugging at the leg of the Master, and singing, "Oh, I am so happy." Did Jesus know that once home and asleep Alma kept crying out in a nightmare of fear that he was still crippled? His mother awakened him and helped him again to his feet. And then tried to laugh through her tears, as he sprang all over the bed saying, "Look! Look what I can do!"

Jesus had wept yesterday. Nephi was weeping now. And feeling all the honest unutterable gratitude of a little child.

Jesus spoke:

"So great faith have I never seen among all the Jews; wherefore I could not show unto them so great miracles, because of their unbelief.

"Verily I say unto you, there are none of them that have seen so great things as ye have seen; neither have they heard so great things as ye have heard."

All was silent. It was a rich, warm silence; the serenity of it seemed charged with peace, and more of love wafted through the air than any sound of motion could carry. This was communion in the manner of the angels. This was holy ground.

Impulsively, still on his knees, Nephi reached to Timothy and embraced his shoulders. In the security of that gesture something passed between them. Both were vividly aware that the sores and scars of their long labor seemed now the tokens of rejoicing. They marveled that they could ever have been wearied, that any strand of their mind or body could have felt the costs too great. For their enemies, even those of murderous intent, they felt a well of forgiveness. Without looking at each other they knew, knew now a whole renewal to endure and to overcome . . . for him . . . like him. An invincible wish pulled at their throats. And as they lifted their heads they wondered if the Savior knew their thoughts.

He knew.